THE ESSENTIAL

TAYLOR SWIFT

FANBOOK

Published in 2023 by Welbeck Children's Books
An imprint of Hachette Children's Group
Part of Hodder and Stoughton
Carmelite House
50 Victoria Embankment
London EC4Y 0DZ
An Hachette UK Company

www.hachette.co.uk
www.hachettechildrens.co.uk

All information correct as of July 2023.

The publishers would like to thank the following sources for their kind permission to reproduce the pictures in this book.

GETTY IMAGES: Isaac Brekken 44-45; Larry Busacca 1, 32BR, 49TR; Gareth Cattermole/TAS 28-29B; Michael Caulfield/AMA 39; Erin Clark/The Boston Globe 26R; Rick Diamond 28TR; Rick Diamond/ACM 6TL; Nina Dietzel 8BL; Kevork Djansezian 41TL; Francois Durand 48BL; Rich Fury 16-17; Jesse D Garrabrant/NBAE 8R; Bruce Glikas/FilmMagic 41BL; Steve Granitz/WireImage 30TR, 38; Raymond Hall/GC Images 6BL, 21L; Frazer Harrison 32BC, 34R; Frazer Harrison/ACMA 40BR; Anthony Harvey 48BR; Taylor Hill/FilmMagic 33TR; Octavio Jones/TAS 34BR, 41BR; Dimitrios Kambouris 33BL, 52-53, 54; Kevin Kane 10TR, 10BRL Kipuxa 20L; Pascal Kiszon 20C; Jon Kopaloff/FilmMagic 48TC; Jeff Kravitz/FilmMagic 9TR, 32BL, 33BC, 41TR, 60; Krissy Krummenacker/MediaNews Group/Reading Eagle 7; Dan MacMedan/WireImage 9BR; Maremagnum 10L; Kevin Mazur 33TC, 49BC, 49BR, 62; Kevin Mazur/TAS 24-25, 27; Kevin Mazur/WireImage 23TR, 30L, 31TR, 31BR, 41C, 56-57; Jamie McCarthy 33TL, 46-47; Emma McIntyre 49BL; Al Messerschmidt 48TL; Mark Metcalfe 50-51; Ethan Miller 35, 58-59; Neil Mockford/FilmMagic 32TR; Sarah Morris/FilmMagic 33BR, 48-49; Cepi Nurdin/500px 20B; Christopher Polk 4-5, 55BR; Christopher Polk/ACMA 6L, 48BC; Christopher Polk/FilmMagic 9L; Christopher Polk/Penske Media 14-15; Christopher Polk/TAS 11TR; Jun Sato/WireImage 29TL; John Shearer 22BL; John Shearer/TAS 2-3, 12-13, 18-19, 26TR, 26BR; John Shearer/WireImage 23L, 30BR; Mindy Small/FilmMagic 55TR; Amy Sussman 11BR; Pierre Suu 31BL; TAS 11L; Michael Tran/FilmMagic 36-37; Jeff Vespa/WireImage 40R; Andrew H Walker 22TL; Angela Weiss/AFP 63; Matt Winkelmeyer/TAS 40L, 42-43; Kevin Winter 22R, 48TR; Terry Wyatt 64; Kevin Mazur/TAS BACK COVER

SHUTTERSTOCK: Olgsera 8BC; Startraks 21R

ALAMY: Casey Flanigan/MediaPunch Inc COVER

ISBN 978 1 83935 288 1

Printed in Dongguan, China

10 9 8 7 6 5 4 3 2

FSC
www.fsc.org
MIX
Paper | Supporting responsible forestry
FSC® C144853

CONTENTS

Welcome

★★★★★★★★★★★★★★★★★★★

Calling all Swifties! This book is bursting with all things Taylor, from fashion and fan guides, to cool collabs and her beloved cats. Besides learning fun facts and taking cool quizzes, you can hang out with Taylor's besties, relive her biggest anthems and melodies, plus try to tally the oodles of awards she's racking up. So, get ready to celebrate the queen of country-pop.

Meet Taylor

Do you call yourself a TayTay superfan? Whether you're a fully-fledged member of the Swifties or new to the party, this is your chance to get to know the gal behind some of the greatest hits in pop history.

MOM AND DAD

AUSTIN

OLIVIA BENSON

Swift Facts

NAME:	**Taylor Alison Swift**
FROM:	**West Reading, Pennsylvania**
DATE OF BIRTH:	**December 13, 1989**
HAIR COLOR:	**Blonde**
EYE COLOR:	**Blue**
STAR SIGN:	**Sagittarius**
MOM:	**Andrea Gardner Swift**
DAD:	**Scott Kingsley Swift**
YOUNGER BROTHER:	**Austin Kingsley Swift**
MUSICAL INSTRUMENTS:	**Guitar, banjo, piano, ukulele**
HOBBIES:	**Making jam and baking**
PET CATS:	**Meredith Grey**
	Olivia Benson
	Benjamin Button

As a little girl, Taylor grew up on her family's Christmas tree farm in Pennsylvania.

How It Started
vs. How It's Going

From a wavy-haired, country-singing teen who came onto the scene in the early 2000s to a sensational superstar with sell-out stadium tours! This is Taylor's journey to stardom...

Taylor's roots

Young Tay lived on a Christmas tree farm and grew up LOVING all things Christmas. But you'll know this already if you've listened to her holiday single, "Christmas Tree Farm." The music video contains super-sweet video clips of a very little Taylor, with her brother and parents, opening presents, sledding, and basically having lots of festive fun!

AGED 12

NASHVILLE

Nashville

Music was important to Taylor from a young age. She started out by singing covers in talent contests, but age at 12, she learned to play guitar and began writing her own songs. As a kid, Taylor REALLY wanted to move to Nashville in Tennessee, where famous country singers like Dolly Parton and Faith Hill had got their big breaks. Taylor was determined to succeed and would tirelessly send her demo tapes to different studios in the hope that someone would sign her.

Big move

When she was 13 years old, Tay's family moved from Pensylvannia to Nashville so that she could follow her music-career dreams. Taylor soon nabbed herself a record deal with Big Machine Records. Just two years later, Taylor released her first album, called *Taylor Swift*, which included the song "Tim McGraw". This track went on to become her first top-40 hit as well as Breakthrough Video of the Year at the 2007 CMT Music Awards.

Fearless

A new level of success came for Taylor in 2008 as she scored her first number 1 album with *Fearless*. That same year, she raised her profile by performing with the mega-popular Jonas Brothers on their Burnin' Up Tour.

JONAS BROTHERS

BIG WINS!

2010 saw Taylor's stardom zoom to new heights when she won big at the Grammys. And we mean BIG... Check it out:

★ **ALBUM OF THE YEAR -** *Fearless*

★ **BEST FEMALE COUNTRY VOCAL PERFORMANCE**

★ **BEST COUNTRY SONG**

★ **BEST COUNTRY ALBUM**

9

Record Breaker

The iconic "We Are Never Ever Getting Back Together" from Taylor's fourth album, *Red*, is one of her most famous singles. In 2012 it broke the record as the fastest-selling digital single ever by a female artist. *Red* was also a big move away from TayTay's country sound.

NEW YORK

Big Apple

In 2014, Taylor left her beloved Nashville behind to move to the Big Apple—New York City. She released her dance-floor filler "Shake It Off," an unforgettable single from her fifth album *1989*. During her *1989* world tour, Taylor began to introduce famous guests appearances at her shows. Celebs included Lisa Kudrow (Phoebe from *Friends*), the actress Julia Roberts and Mick Jagger (lead singer of The Rolling Stones). The tour was mega and got everybody talking!

SHAKE IT OFF

Back With a Bang . . .

After a short break, Taylor came back better than ever (if you can imagine that!) in 2017 with the single "Look What You Made Me Do." It was from her sixth album, *Reputation*. By 2018 she left the record label Big Machine for Republic Records and Universal Music Group.

REPUTATION TOUR

Loving It

Taylor released her seventh album, *Lover*, into the world in 2019. With 18 tracks, this was her longest to date. She released it in the same year that she appeared in the movie adaptation of Andrew Lloyd Webber's *Cats*. Is there nothing this gal can't do? In 2020, Taylor released *Folklore*, her eighth album, which nabbed her another Grammy for Album of the Year. Later that same year, she released her ninth album—*Evermore*.

GRAMMYS PERFORMANCE 2020

Late-Night Inspo

Taylor's tenth album, *Midnights*, was released in 2022 and has a synth-pop sound. Taylor says that it was inspired by sleepless nights and that she even wrote some of the songs in the middle of the night! Ten of the 13 songs occupied the entire top 10 of the US Billboard Hot 100 on its release.

"Happiness and confidence are two of the prettiest things you can wear . . ."

TAYLOR SWIFT

TAYLOR IN NUMBERS

10 ALBUMS RELEASED

"*Anti-Hero*" spent **8 WEEKS** AT **No.1** ON THE US BILLBOARD HOT 100

13 years old AGE TAYLOR SIGNED WITH *her First Record Label*

60 WEEKS AT **NUMBER 1** ON THE US BILLBOARD ARTIST 100 CHART

First female ARTIST TO WIN **ALBUM OF THE YEAR** FOR THE **3rd time** AT THE 2021 GRAMMYS

40 ★

AMERICAN MUSIC AWARDS RECEIVED

9 UK **NUMBER 1** ALBUMS

250 **MILLION** +

INSTAGRAM FOLLOWERS

19 YEARS OLD

AGE TAYLOR BECAME THE YOUNGEST EVER

COUNTRY MUSIC AWARDS **Entertainer of the Year**

13 years old

AGE TAYLOR MOVED TO **NASHVILLE** TO BECOME A *Country Artist*

21 UK **TOP 10** SINGLES

Top Hits and Anthems

Let's celebrate some of Taylor's finest tunes from her beautiful ballads to her "sick beats" plus the songs that made her famous!

TIM MCGRAW

Album: **Taylor Swift**

Year: **2006**

We couldn't not mention this single. This is where it all began after all. This love song is classic Taylor, and it was her first top 10 country hit as well as her first US Billboard Hot 100 chart entry. Taylor was inspired to write this song when she was still at school.

LOVE STORY

Album: **Fearless**

Year: **2008**

When 17-year-old Taylor's parents didn't want her to date a guy, she channeled her frustration into writing this song. It has strong fairy tale vibes (princes and princesses, eat your hearts out!) and those famous lyrics about the forbidden love of Romeo and Juliet.

SHAKE IT OFF

Album: **1989**

Year: **2014**

Love it or hate it, this uber-catchy track is a dance-floor favorite that's guaranteed to get everyone singing and bopping along, no matter who they are. It's the perfect track to rid yourself of negativity! The upbeat song was Taylor's second number 1 hit.

BLANK SPACE

Album: **1989**

Year: **2014**

If it's bangers you're after, then look no further than *Blank Space*! This pop anthem kicks in with a strong beat that makes you want to jump up and sing along. The song makes fun of all the negative stories about Taylor's personal life in the media.

ANTI-HERO

Album: **Midnights**

Year: **2022**

This single is all about self-doubt and feeling insecure, and it totally dominated the charts. Taylor wrote this one with Jack Antonoff, and it went on to top the US Billboard Hot 100 for eight weeks, making it TayTay's longest running number 1 hit... so far.

★

Following the release of her album *Midnights*, Taylor broke the record for the most top 10 hits by a female artist with an incredible 40 of them.

17

10 Reasons We Love Tay

There are SO many reasons, right?
But we've whittled it down to our top 10.

1

FEMINIST ICON
Taylor isn't afraid to speak out about important issues, and feminism is close to her heart. She often shares love for fellow female artists—she's all about lifting people up.

2

DONATES TO CHARITY
From funding wildlife and conservation charities to donating her autographed guitar to PETA, Taylor spreads the word about charities she cares about.

3

SHOWS LOVE FOR FANS
Whether she's offering advice to them on social media or thanking them for her success, Taylor is constantly showing her fans the love and that she never takes them for granted!

4

DEDICATED CAT MOMMA
She is one proud cat parent to her beloved feline friends, and she takes them everywhere. More about her fur babies on page 20!

5

WRITES HER OWN SONGS
Not only does Taylor write her own chart-topping hits, but she writes them for other artists, too, like Calvin Harris.

6

DIRECTS MUSIC VIDEOS
The first music video Taylor directed was for her 2019 track, "The Man." This gal proves you really can do it all, and she bosses it every time!

7 SHE'S HONEST
Besides writing songs about her life and experiences, Taylor has also talked openly about being lonely and finding school tough because she didn't have many friends.

8 THE DANCE MOVES!
Taylor dances like nobody is watching. When she moves, it's all about having fun and not at all about trying to look cool! It's the best way.

9 HER FRIENDS ARE #SQUADGOALS
Yup, hands down, TayTay's got THE coolest girl gang, and we all want to be a part of it.

10 SHE IS GROUNDED
Even though she's one of the biggest popstars ever, Taylor hasn't let it go to her head. She still gets super excited about the things she gets to do!

Pet Corner

All you Swifties out there will know that TayTay has three fabulous and furry family members who she talks about . . . A LOT. Taylor takes her role as Cat Mom very seriously, and we're here for it. Get ready for cuteness overload!

CAT "SQUAD"

NAME: Meredith Grey
BREED: Scottish fold
ADOPTED: 2011
NAMED AFTER:
Meredith Grey from
Grey's Anatomy

A SCOTTISH FOLD CAT

Both Ellen Pompeo who played Meredith Grey in *Grey's Anatomy* and Mariska Hargitay who played Olivia Benson in *Law and Order: SVU* appear in Taylor's "Bad Blood" music video.

A SCOTTISH FOLD CAT

NAME: Olivia Benson
BREED: Scottish fold
ADOPTED: 2014
NAMED AFTER:
Olivia Benson from
Law and Order: SVU

NAME: Button
BREED: Ragdoll
ADOPTED: 2019
NAMED AFTER:
Benjamin Button in the movie of the same name

A RAGDOLL CAT

Paw-fect Match

We met Benjamin when he appeared in Taylor's music video for *"Me!"* In fact, that's where Taylor met him too! It was love at first sight—Taylor adopted him, and the rest is history.

First-Class Passengers

Taylor's cats go everywhere with her, and they sure travel in style.

OLIVIA

MEREDITH

Career Kitty

It turns out Olivia has a career to rival any human's and has made it onto the 2023 Pet Rich List. From cameos in Taylor's music videos to a successful career in commercials, Olivia even has her own merchandise! So extra.

Plus Two

A-list events are a go for Meredith and Olivia, who were Tay's dates at the 2019 Billboard Music Awards. They really are living the dream!

The Squad

It's the team all Swifties dream of being part of—Taylor and her famous girl gang are absolute squad goals!

Blake Lively

The pair have been friends for years, and they are very close. Taylor even thanked Blake and her family in her speech when she won Album of the Year for *Folklore*.

Emma Stone

The friendship began when they both attended the Young Hollywood Awards in 2008, where they hit it off. Since then, Tay has accompanied Emma to one of her movie premieres, and Emma has come along to some of Taylor's tours.

Lorde

Taylor sent flowers to Lorde when she released her first ever single, "Royals." This act of kindness led to them meeting up and becoming pals.

Gigi Hadid

This duo has been BFFs since they met at an event in 2014. Gigi was one of the pals featured in Taylor's famous "Bad Blood" music video. Gigi tries to make it to as many of Taylor's shows as she can and sometimes even joins Tay on stage.

Selena Gomez

This friendship started when Taylor and Selena were both dating Jonas brothers (Joe and Nick) in 2008. Although the relationships ended, the girls have stayed friends. Taylor has been to Selena's movie premieres, they hang out at awards shows together, and they've even sung together.

All About the Eras Tour

If you're lucky enough to nab tickets, Taylor's current tour takes you through all her musical eras and celebrates all her studio albums so far.

44 SONGS
IN THE SET LIST, TAKEN FROM **10 ALBUMS**

★★★★★★★★★★★★★★★★★★★★★

THESE TRACKS REPRESENT THE **10 "ERAS" OF TAYLOR**

8 HOURS
HOW LONG U.S. FANS QUEUED ONLINE TO GET TICKETS

MARCH 2023
DATE THE **ERAS TOUR** DEBUTED IN THE US

TAYLOR'S FIRST TOUR
SINCE THE **REPUTATION** STADIUM TOUR IN **2018**

Taylor Sings
TWO SURPRISE
ACOUSTIC TRACKS DURING EACH SHOW

★★★★★★★★★★★★★★★★★

SHE USUALLY TREATS FANS TO A **SPECIAL GUEST** TO HELP WITH THIS PART

★

"I don't know how to process how you all are making me feel right now."

Taylor Swift on her opening night

TOP 5 Eras Tour Moments

Like you'd expect, there are A LOT of them, but here are some not to be missed!

PHOEBE BRIDGERS

Taylor throwbacks

Her dancers are a highlight of any Taylor show. Well, this tour is no different. When Tay performs "Look What You Made Me Do," her dancers don some of Taylor's iconic looks from yesteryear.

Marjorie's moment

Expect all the feels. The performance of her song "Marjorie" about her late Grandma is guaranteed to get the crowds teary-eyed and waving their phone lights in time to the music.

Bracelet swap

Trading friendship bracelets is a cute idea that Tay's fans have embraced to the max. Fans at the Eras Tour are trading friendship bracelets, linking themselves to others who shared the same incredible experience.

THAT dive

Nobody could have predicted the moment Taylor dives into a pool of water at the front of the stage. She then appears to swim underwater! It's a breathtaking moment and one that must be seen to be believed!

Special guests

We all know how Tay loves to bring out a surprise guest and the Eras Tour is no different. So far, she's brought out the likes of Marcus Mumford, Phoebe Bridgers, and Aaron Dessner.

"The most miraculous process is watching a song go from a tiny idea in the middle of the night to something that 55,000 people are singing back to you."

TAYLOR SWIFT

Fans ♥ Taylor

When it comes to showing appreciation for her fans, Taylor does not hold back. Think surprise wedding appearances, handwritten letters, and love advice!

SHE STICKS UP FOR THEM

When TayTay saw a fan being yelled at by security at her concert, she stopped singing to defend them. The Swifties were just dancing, and for some reason, this security guard didn't like it. The security guard was then asked to leave, and the fan and her friends were given free tickets to the gig.

SHE WRITES HER FANS HANDWRITTEN LETTERS

Tay takes the time to reply to her fans with letters. And they're not just typed form letters either—they're personalized and handwritten. Even more special, they're often decorated with her beautiful watercolor paintings.

SHE SHOWS UP AT THEIR WEDDINGS

How could your big day get even bigger? Invite Taylor Swift. Yep, she turned up to surprise one of her superfans on their wedding day. Not only did Taylor sing her hit "Blank Space" while playing the piano, but she even painted the couple a watercolor card featuring the lyric "so it's gonna be forever."

SHE GIVES THEM ADVICE ON SOCIAL MEDIA

Lots of fans message their idols on Instagram never expecting their hero to see it, let alone reply. But Taylor isn't like most popstars! Over the years, she's thrilled fans with brilliant replies and helpful advice. Let's be honest, she's like the big sister we all want!

Cool Collabs

Just like all of Tay's musical decisions, her choice of artists to work with are always top-notch. Here are some of the A-listers that are proud to be Team Taylor.

Haim

This friendship has been a long-running one. Back in 2015, the Haim sisters joined Tay on her *1989* World Tour. They also collaborated on Taylor's 2020 *Evermore* album on the track called "No Body, No Crime." In 2022, Taylor joined the Haim girls at London's O2 Arena. Together the fierce foursome performed a mashup of "Love Song" from Taylor's *Fearless* album, along with a rendition of "Gasoline."

Lana Del Rey

Have you heard "Snow on the Beach" yet? If not, you need to fix that pronto. This beautiful track from Taylor's *Midnights* album features Lana Del Rey. Taylor is always shouting out about how much she admires Lana's music and what an amazing talent she is.

Miley Cyrus

Taylor and Miley sang together at the 51st Grammys in 2009. The unstoppable gals belted out a stripped-back rendition of Taylor's song "Fifteen." Check it out for a throwback to old-school Taylor (and Miley too!), harmonies galore, and Taylor rocking it on her guitar.

Kendrick Lamar

In her infamous "Bad Blood" track, Taylor collaborated with hip-hop royalty, Kendrick Lamar. But before they got to this point, the pair had talked openly about how they admired one another's music and even shared videos singing or lip-syncing each other's songs. Love it!

Sir Paul McCartney

Taylor met with Sir Paul McCartney (of The Beatles) for *Rolling Stone* magazine in 2020, to talk about their music. It turns out that Taylor's relationship with her young fans inspired Paul McCartney's song, "Who Cares."

Ed Sheeran

Besides being good mates for a long time, Ed and Taylor enjoy making music together. Ed collaborated with Taylor on three of her songs: "Everything Has Changed" (*Red* album), "End Game" (*Reputation* album), and "Run" (*Red: Taylor's version*). Taylor was then on a remix of Ed's "The Joker and the Queen" track.

Taylor's Style Evolution

Looking good! Check out TayTay's fashion choices from cute curls and cowboy boots to bold blazers and bodysuits.

BERET CHIC Keeping it cool and classic with a bold red beret and natural waves.

BELLE OF THE BALL Giving off princess vibes at the Grammys in this lilac bodice.

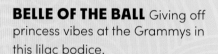

2008

2006

COUNTRY CUTENESS

Throwback to the early days of Taylor sporting halters and cowboy boots.

2016

MONOCHROME MINI

Now, that's how you make a statement—black lips, bleached hair, and a cut-out mini dress.

TARTAN TWO-PIECE Matching sets have become a signature Swift style!

2014

BOHO BABE Big sleeves, pastel shades, and delicate floral detailing—what's not to love?

2019

2021

HOLLYWOOD GLAM

Big bouncy waves and a gold-studded catsuit. No. Words.

2022

2021

FLOWER POWER

Bringing all the spring vibes with a floral explosion of a dress.

2019

TAILORED TAYLOR

Taylor looked the business in this super-luxe, velvet blazer.

COLOR POP Going for bold with this graphic blazer with shoulder pads. Iconic!

What's Your Taylor Look?

Taylor's mastered heaps of awesome looks over the years, but which one is most you? Take this quiz and jot down your answers to reveal all.

1 Pick a hairstyle:
- **A.** French plaits
- **B.** Big, bouncy curls
- **C.** Ringlets

2 Pick an accessory:
- **A.** Flower crown
- **B.** Gold bracelet and rings
- **C.** Hoop earrings

3 In a school play, you'd prefer to be...
- **A.** Making the costumes
- **B.** Acting the main part
- **C.** Playing a musical instrument

4 You're choosing an outfit for a big event. Which kind of dress would you go for?
- **A.** Something feminine and floral
- **B.** Anything with sequins
- **C.** A cute halter

5 What's your favorite way to spend a Saturday?
- **A.** Beach trip
- **B.** Cinema
- **C.** Country walk

Your dream holiday would be a...
A. Fab festival
B. City getaway
C. Outdoor adventure

6

Choose a weekend activity:
A. Reading a good book
B. Going out on the town with my besties
C. Writing music

7

Which is your favorite subject at school?
A. Art
B. Drama
C. Music

8

In your friendship group, you're the...
A. Listener
B. Leader
C. Chill one

9

When you grow up, you'd rather be a...
A. Artist
B. Movie star
C. Musician

10

MOSTLY A's
Your Taylor style is BOHO BABE.
Teaming pretty, floaty dresses with your loose waves is your signature style, and the best part is that you make it look effortless! You love daisy chains, flower crowns, and ditsy detailing.

MOSTLY B's
Your Taylor style is HOLLYWOOD GLAM.
There's nothing low-key about your look, and that's why everyone loves it. It doesn't matter if you're going for a milkshake or dressing up for a party, you know how to bring silver-screen glamor to any outfit. Bring on the sparkly sequins and shine!

MOSTLY C's
Your Taylor style is COUNTRY CUTENESS.
You're happiest in denim, plaid, and casual halter dresses. This was Taylor's vibe when the world first caught a glimpse of her! Just like TayTay, whatever you wear, you always manage to put your own unique stamp on it. Cowboy boots for the win!

★

"Just be yourself; there is no one better."

TAYLOR SWIFT

TayTay's Trophy Case

Nobody can deny that this country-turned-pop singer rocks the awards season each year. Here are some of her biggest wins to date and counting . . .

12x
MTV EUROPE AWARDS

FOR 2022 ALONE, TAY WON . . .

★ Best Video and Best Longform Video for "All Too Well" (10 Minute Version)

★ Best Artist   ★ Best Pop

Taylor is tied with Lady Gaga as the singer with the most MTV EUROPE AWARDS.

29x
BILLBOARD MUSIC AWARDS

★ Top Artist **2015**

★ Top Selling Album **2018**

★ Top Country Album for her version of *Red* **2022**

14x
MTV VIDEO MUSIC AWARDS

★ "Bad Blood" **2015**
★ "You Need to Calm Down" **2019**
★ "All Too Well" (10 Minute Version) **2021**

She is the only artist to win the MTV VIDEO OF THE YEAR three times...

NICKELODEON KIDS' CHOICE AWARDS

FOR 2023 ALONE, TAY WON...

★ Favorite Female Artist
★ Favorite Album for *Midnights (3am Edition)*

12x
GRAMMY AWARDS

HIGHLIGHTS INCLUDE . . .

★ Album of the Year (for *Fearless, 1989* and *Folklore*)
★ Best Music Video (for "Bad Blood")
★ Best Female Country Vocal Performance (for "White Horse")

Taylor's cat **OLIVIA BENSON** was named 2023 Favorite Celebrity Pet
NICKELODEON KIDS' CHOICE AWARDS

40x
AMERICAN MUSIC AWARDS

HIGHLIGHTS INCLUDE . . .

★ Favorite Country Female Artist
★ Artist of the Decade **2019**
★ Artist of the Year **2020**

5 YEARS IN A ROW!
Favorite Country Female Artist
AMERICAN MUSIC AWARDS

8 songs You Didn't Know Were By Taylor

As if the back catalog of her own hits aren't enough, Taylor has been writing for movies and major artists, too!

Hannah Montana (movie)

Miley sang "You'll Always Find Your Way Back Home" in the 2009 movie *Hannah Montana: The Movie*. But you may not know that it was written by Taylor Swift along with a singer called Martin Johnson. Taylor also put in a star performance in the movie when she sang "Crazier."

Sugarland

The American country music duo, Sugarland, have a song called "Babe" that was written by Taylor and Patrick Monahan.

Little Big Town

"Better Man" was released by Little Big Town in 2016, and it was a huge hit—so huge that it even won Song of the Year at the Country Music Awards in 2017. The country band have a lot to thank Taylor for, seeing as she wrote the song and sent it to them. Taylor also sings the song on her album *Red (Taylor's Version)*.

Calvin Harris

Remember that Calvin Harris banger "This Is What You Came For?" The song featured Rihanna and was written by Taylor when she and Calvin were dating. The pair chose to keep this on the down-low as they thought it could be a distraction for fans.

Hunger Games (movie)

Along with The Civil Wars band, Tay co-wrote "Safe and Sound" from the *Hunger Games* movie soundtrack. As well as this track, one of Taylor's own songs *Eyes Open* also made its way onto the movie soundtrack.

Boys Like Girls

Taylor wrote "Two Is Better Than One" with singer-songwriter Martin Johnson for his band Boys Like Girls.

Big Red Machine

Taylor teamed up with The National / Big Red Machine's Aaron Dessner to write the track "Renegade". She also sings on the song!

Cats (the movie)

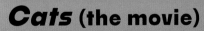

It's no surprise that a cat obsessive like TayTay would want to get involved with the *Cats* movie. Not only did she star in it as a feline called Bombalurina, but she also co-wrote the movie's theme song "Beautiful Ghosts" with Andrew Lloyd Webber.

Our 5 Favorite Music Videos

It's hard to choose a top 5 from all of Tay's outstanding offerings, but we managed it!

BEST DANCE MOVES

You Belong With Me
(from the album *Fearless*)

There's a lot to love about this one. It's fun, it's endearing, and it's all about championing the underdog. It's that classic teen romcom set-up with cheerleaders versus nerds, love notes galore, and even a prom! Taylor plays two parts—the nerd who dances like nobody's watching, plus the popular girl with the car and boyfriend. The main message is to embrace your inner nerd and don't change to be liked.

Bad Blood (from the album *1989*)

This notorious music video has a big celeb ensemble, like seriously BIG. We're talking about Zendaya, Hailee Steinfeld, Cara Delevingne, Kendrick Lamar, Cindy Crawford, Karlie Kloss, and Selena Gomez to name but a few. When this song comes on, you wake up and pay attention! The video has stunts aplenty, which the multi-talented Taylor performed herself.

BEST CAMEOS!

BEST STORYTELLING

Blank Space (from the album *1989*)

Released in 2015, "Blank Space" was co-written by Taylor and is set in an epic mansion. We love her costumes, her ace acting skills, and then there's the beautiful white horses. And of course, her cat Olivia makes an appearance. Taylor's storytelling skills shine bright in this video, which is bursting with drama and has over three billion views on YouTube. It also won MTV Video Music Awards for Best Female Video and Best Pop Video.

MOST
BEAUTIFUL

Wildest Dreams
(from the album *1989*)

We cannot talk about this video without mentioning the stunning setting. It was filmed in Africa, with amazing lions, giraffes, and beautiful waterfalls. The song is about remembering the good things in a relationship after it ends. In the video, Taylor is a glamorous fifties actress on a movie set. Oh, and THAT yellow dress? It's everything.

MOST
EMPOWERING

The Man
(from the album *Lover*)

In "The Man," Taylor questions what it would be like to be a male in the music industry and how differently she'd be treated. This feminist anthem has an awesome video to boot, and it was the first music video that Taylor ever directed (many have followed since!). It was nominated for three MTV Music Awards, including Video of the Year, Video for Good, and Best Direction—it won Best Direction!

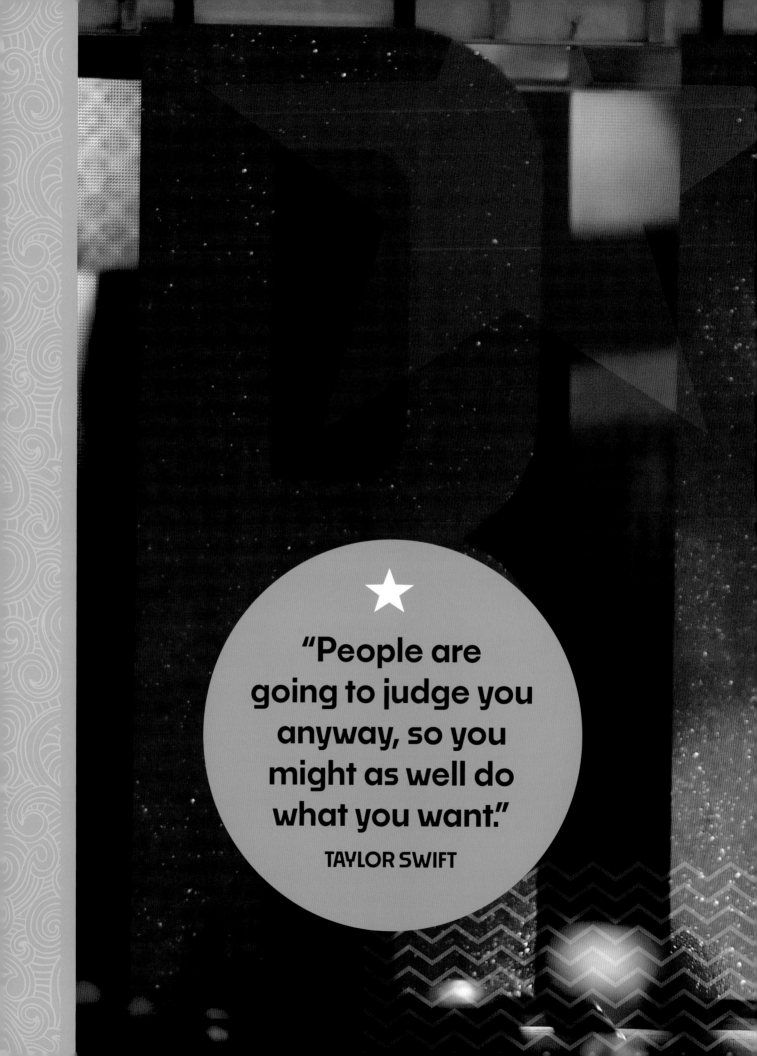

"People are going to judge you anyway, so you might as well do what you want."

TAYLOR SWIFT

10 Things You Didn't Know About Taylor

Read on and impress your crew with your super-Swiftie know-how.

1 She's still BFFs with Abigail—the friend mentioned in "Fifteen," remember?

2 Ten-year-old Taylor wrote a poem called "Monster In My Closet" and won a national poetry contest.

3 Tay was a model for Abercrombie & Fitch in 2003, just like Jennifer Lawrence, Emma Roberts, and Channing Tatum.

4 Taylor was taught to play guitar by a computer repairman.

5 TayTay's favorite TV show is *Friends*.

6 Horse-riding was a big part of Taylor's childhood. She competed until she was 12 years old.

7 We all know Tay writes her own songs, but she wrote the entire *Speak Now* album totally solo—not even one co-writer in sight!

8 She's named after American singer-songwriter James Taylor. This legendary guitarist has won six Grammys and is one of the best-selling artists of all time.

9 Taylor's grandmother, Marjorie, was an opera singer. Tay even wrote a song called "Marjorie" for her.

10 Tay paints a 13 on her hand before every show she plays. It's her lucky number and for good reasons—she was born on 13 December, her first album went gold in 13 weeks, and she was once sat in row 13 when she won an award.

We're Hair For It!

Let's take time to reflect on some highlights of Taylor's golden tresses.

Who remembers this super sweet look? Back in 2006, fresh-faced Taylor had a head of bouncy blonde waves.

We love this sophisticated style. Tay looks all kinds of elegant with this up-do!

Taylor was all about the Hollywood glamor with her fifties-style curls for this memorable MTV Music Awards' performance in 2010.

Blunt bangs has become one of Taylor's signature hairstyles! We love her 2013 full fringe with long locks.

Bob + side-swept bangs = volume! What's not to love?

Looking sharp at the 2016 Grammys with this blunt bob and soft bangs combo.

Hands up who loved Tay's bleach-blonde shaggy crop!

Could she look any edgier? TayTay glows with beautiful highlights and soft waves.

This simple, sophisticated style screams, "Taylor means business" . . . although when doesn't she, right?

Check out Taylor's Abba-style feathered bangs. Obsessed.

49

11 Signs You're a Taylor Superfa[n]

Calling all Swifties . . . how many of these sound like you?

1 You know every single word to every single one of her songs.

2 Like all true fans, you've sent her fan mail. We all know how Taylor loves receiving letters!

3 She inspired you to write. You keep a diary and jot down poems or songs about your life, what you do and how you feel.

4 You can name all the members of her squad. All of them! A pal of Taylor's is a pal of yours.

5 If you overhear someone singing her lyrics incorrectly, you HAVE to correct them!

6 Whenever you hum a tune, it's guaranteed to be one of TayTay's.

7 You follow her pets' careers closely.

8 You took guitar lessons so you could be more like your hero.

9 You quote her without realizing you're even doing it.

10 You have one of her song lyrics stored up for every occasion.

11 If Tay says she likes an artist or group, you go give them a listen. No questions asked!

How to Write Songs the Swift Way

The songstress has shared many tips about her songwriting process over the years. Here's what we've learned...

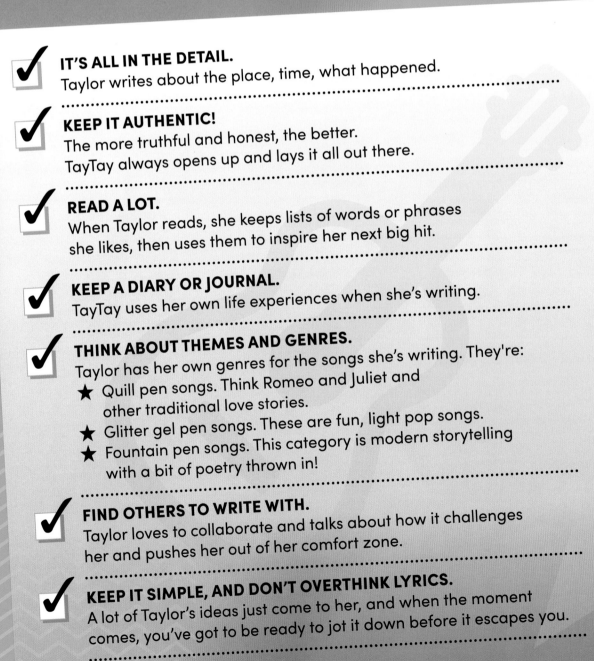

✔ **IT'S ALL IN THE DETAIL.**
Taylor writes about the place, time, what happened.

✔ **KEEP IT AUTHENTIC!**
The more truthful and honest, the better.
TayTay always opens up and lays it all out there.

✔ **READ A LOT.**
When Taylor reads, she keeps lists of words or phrases she likes, then uses them to inspire her next big hit.

✔ **KEEP A DIARY OR JOURNAL.**
TayTay uses her own life experiences when she's writing.

✔ **THINK ABOUT THEMES AND GENRES.**
Taylor has her own genres for the songs she's writing. They're:
★ Quill pen songs. Think Romeo and Juliet and other traditional love stories.
★ Glitter gel pen songs. These are fun, light pop songs.
★ Fountain pen songs. This category is modern storytelling with a bit of poetry thrown in!

✔ **FIND OTHERS TO WRITE WITH.**
Taylor loves to collaborate and talks about how it challenges her and pushes her out of her comfort zone.

✔ **KEEP IT SIMPLE, AND DON'T OVERTHINK LYRICS.**
A lot of Taylor's ideas just come to her, and when the moment comes, you've got to be ready to jot it down before it escapes you.

"Writing songs is my life's work, my hobby, and my never-ending thrill. I am moved beyond words that you, my peers, decided to honor me in this way for work I'd still be doing if I had never been recognized for it."

TAYLOR SWIFT

"Know the person you are writing the songs about . . .Then write a letter to them—what you would say if you could? That's why I listen to music. It says how I feel better than I could. And it says what I wished I had said when that moment was there."

TAYLOR SWIFT

How Well Do You Know Tay?

Call yourself a Swiftie? Grab a pen and some paper and get ready to test your Taylor knowledge!

1 What is Taylor's lucky number?

2 Which member of Taylor's family was an opera singer?

3 Name Taylor's first album.

4 What is Taylor's favorite TV show?

5 What instrument did Taylor learn to play when she was 12?

6 Which album did Taylor write entirely by herself?

7 What type of farm did Taylor grow up on?

8 What single became Taylor's first top 40 hit?

9 Name all three of her cats.

10 What movie did Taylor write "You'll Always Find Your Way Back Home" for?

11 How old was Taylor when she wrote the poem "Monster In My Closet"?

12 Which movie did Taylor play a cat called Bombalurina in?

13 Where did Taylor and her family move to when she was 13?

Silver-Screen Star

As if dominating the music world wasn't enough, TayTay has also been a shining star in the film industry. Here are some of her starring roles... so far!

Hannah Montana: The Movie 2009

Taylor performed an original song called "Crazier" in this movie starring the one and only Miley Cyrus. Taylor's other songwriting cred on the soundtrack: "You'll Always Find Your Way Back Home."

The Lorax 2012

In this animation of Dr Seuss' *The Lorax*, Taylor voiced a teenager called Audrey. Zac Efron was another famous voice in the movie. He played teenager Ted.

Valentine's Day 2010

Starring as Felicia alongside *Twilight*'s Taylor Lautner, this movie was Taylor's first acting role in a feature film. The two Taylors played characters who were boyfriend and girlfriend on screen, and then the stars began dating in real life, earning their cute coupling the nickname "Taylor Squared." Taylor's song on the soundtrack: "Today Was a Fairytale."

The Giver 2014

Taylor's role may be small in this adaptation of Lois Lowry's book of the same name, but her muiscal talent is showcased in flashbacks, where she's playing the piano.

Cats 2019

Taylor played a furry feline in the movie adaptation of Sir Andrew Lloyd Webber's musical *Cats*. She perfected a British accent for her character Bombalurina, and delivered her song about the infamous bad cat, Macavity, while lying on a floating, sparkly moon. Taylor's song on the soundtrack: "Beautiful Ghost."

All Too Well 2021

Taylor wrote and directed this short movie, which is accompanied by her song of the same name. Multi-tasking and multi-talented TayTay also plays a supporting role in the movie—an older version of the character played by *Stranger Things* star Sadie Sink.

Amsterdam 2022

Swift is part of the star-studded cast of *Amsterdam*, appearing with the very talented Christian Bale, John David Washington, and Margot Robbie.

Other times Taylor features on movie soundtracks:

"Carolina"
for *Where the Crawdads Sing*

"Safe and Sound"
for *The Hunger Games*

"Message in a Bottle"
and "Bad Blood"
for *DC League of Super-Pets*

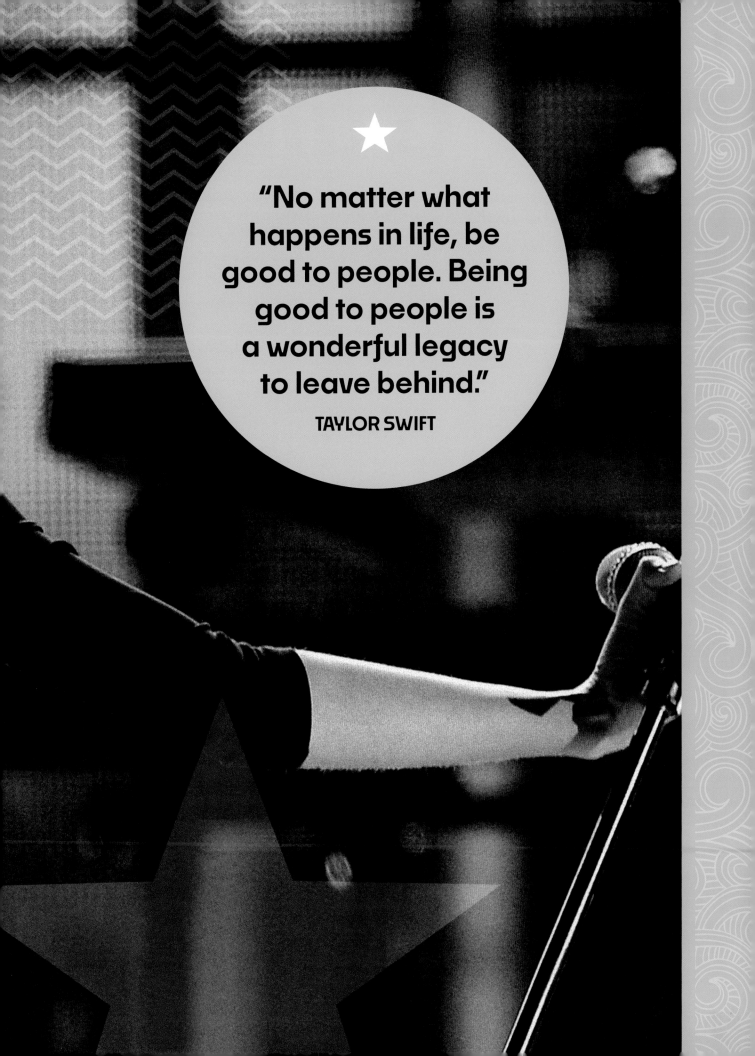

"No matter what happens in life, be good to people. Being good to people is a wonderful legacy to leave behind."

TAYLOR SWIFT

Fan Guide

Want to be Taylor's number one fan?
Here's how you do it.

1 Set yourself a challenge to learn all the lyrics to your fave Taylor songs.

2 Share your love of Taylor with your pals. We're sure they won't need much convincing! You could even start up your own fan club.

3 Put some pics of her up on your bedroom wall. Don't own any? Grab some paper and pens and create your own.

4 Listen to Tay's music in order, starting with her first album *Taylor Swift*. This may take some time since there are 10 of them!

5 Give writing your own songs a try. Taylor was writing for a long time before the world knew who she was.

6 Always big up your friends when they do well, rather than getting jealous about their success.

7 Make up a dance routine to your favorite song. Make sure you get your pals involved, too.

8 Send Taylor some fan mail (just in case you haven't already!). You never know—she may just write back!

9 Learn as many facts about Taylor as you can—this book is an excellent place to start.

10 At your next sleepover, treat yourself and your pals to one of her movies and plenty of popcorn.

11 Be more Taylor and surprise your family, friends, and neighbors with random acts of kindness. You could write them a handwritten letter or bake cookies for them.

12 And last, but not least, lend this book to a fellow Swiftie. Not only is it a kind thing to do, but it also means you'll have someone to talk all things Taylor with. Just make sure they give it back!

Doing Good

From donating to food banks to supporting animal charities, Tay reminds us all of the importance of standing up for what you believe in.

★ Taylor's generosity and dedication to charity has not gone unnoticed. In 2012 she received The Big Help Award from Michelle Obama.

UNICEF

Along with lots of other famous faces, Taylor donated tap water from her own home to UNICEF's Tap Project. People had a chance to win water from their favorite celebs, which helped raise money for people who can't access clean water.

Food banks

While on The Eras tour, Swift made anonymous donations to food banks in every city she visited.

Animal foundation

Taylor made sure money from her "Wildest Dreams" music video went to African Parks Foundation of America. The nonprofit works to conserve vital park lands, protect wildlife, and end poaching.

Taylor uses her platform to talk about issues that are important to her. She's especially passionate about women's rights and the need for LGBTQ equality. You don't need to look too far to find lyrics in her songs that are proudly feminist, plus empowering for people from the LGBTQ community. She even created a petition for fans to sign in order to get the US Senate to support the Equality Act.

"I want to still have a sharp pen, a thin skin, and an open heart."

TAYLOR SWIFT